THE CRYPTO BULL RUN:

How To Make Money From It + 20 Must-Have Coin$ In Your Crypto Portfolio

The Biggest Crypto Bull Run For Generational Wealth Transfer Is Here!!! The Exact Year Is Between 2024 And 2025. Maximize It Fully.

Luther L. Jones

TABLE OF CONTENTS

Introduction

My notion for producing this book derives from my experience with the cryptocurrency market's 2021 bull run. I aim to enhance investor understanding in the cryptocurrency domain before the next bull run occurs, guaranteeing that people comprehend its dynamics and can benefit from its potential returns. This event, which happens every four years, gives huge opportunities for savvy investors.

On June 4, 2021, I started a community focused on empowering individuals with Bitcoin knowledge and education. Prior to this, I had acquired insight into the workings of the crypto bull market via my own cryptocurrency-only transactions. Reflecting on my experience, I recall getting Bitcoin in 2015 at a price of $350. Over the years, I've witnessed its value grow to thousands of dollars, illustrating the immense potential of the cryptocurrency business. Despite widespread criticism of cryptocurrencies, including being labelled as scams and facing government restrictions, a tiny group of savvy investors spotted their long-term financial potential.

These investors, like me, seized the opportunity to gather Bitcoin, expecting its future increase and large profits.

I taught my community about cryptocurrencies, supporting them in comprehending various terms, and we all invested in a range of coins together. Following the acquisition of a new phone, one woman trusted me to handle her crypto portfolio. With a $100 initial investment, we acquired ten cryptocurrency coins worth ten dollars each. To our astonishment, one of these currencies, the Pig Token, surged from $10 to $640 in a relatively short amount of time. The market was humming with exhilaration as coins soared, resulting in substantial profits. It was a remarkable sight—the market was rising during the bull run, pushing people to embrace cryptocurrencies. However, many others missed out on significant returns because they purchased at expensive prices. It was evident that good preparation in collecting coins previous to the bull run was important for maximizing earnings.

Having immersed myself in the domain of cryptocurrencies since mid-2016, I've watched its ebbs and flows, making me something of a seasoned player. I remember the enthusiasm when Bitcoin crossed the $1000 barrier, only to drop by 90% within a few months. I giggled at the Meme tokens called 'shit coins' and observed the surprising growth of the Shiba inu coin in October 2021, it was huge.

All my mentees were reaching out to convey their delight about the remarkable increases their Shiba inu coins were making. One lady, who originally invested $100, had her investment inflate to over $1500 in returns. Another mentee, who got in on the coin at its initial stage, made an incredible $150,000 return. Such is the essence of the crypto market—it goes parabolic during the bull run, giving astonishing rewards to those who take the chance. Despite the time committed to this area, I wouldn't modify a single moment. My view is solid and unwavering: I think that more people will accumulate fortunes via Crypto than any other asset class in years to come. Therefore, I think this book will act as a catalyst for good change in your own financial life. Now we are waiting for the next Bull Run coming in 2025, that's precisely four years after the previous bull run in 2021. You don't want to miss what is coming. This is the opportunity to load your bags with gem tokens at a reasonable cost. This book will help you make educated choices about cryptocurrencies to invest in. It's not financial advice, it's always wise to perform your own research when it comes to any sort of investing.

Also included as a bonus for buying this book are 20 Coins which have been technically evaluated. These currencies should form part of your crypto portfolio. These coins will make you more wealthier than you are today. They are just coins of tremendous worth and profit. I call them the **20 Crypto Gems.**

Chapter 1

What is Bitcoin Halving

Bitcoin halving is a pre-programmed event in the Bitcoin protocol that happens typically every four years, or when every 210,000 blocks are mined. During a halving event, the reward that miners earn for verifying and adding new transactions to the blockchain is slashed in half. This method is meant to manage the issuance pace of new bitcoins and guarantee that the total quantity of bitcoins steadily approaches its predefined ceiling of 21 million coins. The halving mechanism preserve scarcity and has been connected with large price swings in the Bitcoin market.

Bitcoin halving is an event that happens typically every four years in which the amount of new Bitcoin that is created with each block mined is slashed in half. This is done to limit the quantity of Bitcoin and prevent the cryptocurrency from expanding too rapidly. The first Bitcoin halving happened in 2012, while the second halving occurred in 2016. The most recent halving happened on May 11, 2020, decreasing the block reward from 12.5 BTC to 6.25 BTC.

The next Bitcoin halving is scheduled to occur in 2024, about four years after the most recent halving. The precise timing of the next halving is not known as it relies on the pace of Bitcoin mining, which might vary depending on the number of miners and the complexity of the mining algorithm. After the next halving, the block reward will be decreased to 3.125 BTC, and this process will continue every four years until all 21 million Bitcoin has been mined. As the supply of Bitcoin grows scarcer, the value of the cryptocurrency may climb, making it a potentially interesting investment for anyone trying to diversify their portfolio.

Bitcoin halving is a pre-programmed event in the Bitcoin protocol that happens typically every four years, or when every 210,000 blocks are mined. During a halving event, the reward that miners earn for verifying and adding new transactions to the blockchain is slashed in half. This method is meant to manage the issuance pace of new bitcoins and guarantee that the total quantity of bitcoins steadily approaches its predefined ceiling of 21 million coins. The halving mechanism helps preserve scarcity and has traditionally been connected with large price swings in the Bitcoin market.

IMPACT OF BITCOIN HALVING IN THE CRYPTO MARKET

The advantages of Bitcoin halving are mostly connected to the long-term health and stability of the Bitcoin network. By lowering the quantity of new Bitcoins entering circulation, the halving serves to preserve the scarcity and value of the current Bitcoins. This might possibly lead to a rise in the price of Bitcoin since the limited supply of new coins can generate greater demand for old coins.

The effect of Bitcoin halving on the cryptocurrency market might be enormous. The halving may generate a feeling of scarcity and urgency among investors and dealers, which can lead to greater purchasing activity and higher prices. However, the impact may not be immediate, since the market sometimes takes time to completely react to the lower supply. The impact of the halving on other currencies and tokens might vary. Some may suffer a similar surge in demand and price, as investors seek alternate assets to Bitcoin. Others may witness a reduction in demand as investors turn their emphasis to Bitcoin.

For cryptocurrency traders and investors, the perks of Bitcoin halving might include the possibility of better returns on investment. If the price of Bitcoin rises as a consequence of the halving, people who own Bitcoin or invest in Bitcoin-related assets may see their investments improve in value. However, it is crucial to realize that investing in cryptocurrencies may be dangerous and unpredictable, and there is no assurance of profits. It is crucial to perform comprehensive research and understand the hazards before investing in any cryptocurrency.

Chapter 2

What is Crypto Bull Run

A "bull run" is a word used in financial markets, particularly the stock market and cryptocurrency market, to denote a persistent period of increasing prices. It denotes a market where investors are enthusiastic, confident, and purchasing assets with the hope that their prices will continue to grow. The name "bull" stems from the way a bull charges, throwing its horns skyward, suggesting an upward increase in values. A bull run is often characterized by growing trade volumes, favorable market mood, and greater investor engagement.

A crypto bull run refers to a period of continuous price gains in the cryptocurrency market, often accompanied by growing investor confidence and greater trading volumes. During a bull run, values of different cryptocurrencies tend to increase, frequently hitting new all-time highs. These times are frequently driven by good market sentiment, such as rising adoption, favorable regulatory changes, or growing interest from institutional investors.

Bull Market Prediction

This often refers to an anticipation that the financial markets will have a protracted period of increasing asset values. In a bull market, investor confidence is strong, and there's broad optimism about the future performance of stocks or other financial instruments. Predicting a bull market entails examining multiple economic data, market movements, and other elements to predict good market circumstances. However, it's vital to approach market projections with care, since they are fundamentally unreliable and may be altered by unanticipated occurrences by unanticipated events.

How long a bull run lasts

The length of a bull run in financial markets, including the cryptocurrency market, may vary. Bull runs may continue anywhere from a few weeks to many months or even years, depending on several variables such as market circumstances, investor confidence etc. Some bull runs are short-lived, seeing fast price rises followed by abrupt declines, while others may be more extended and persistent. It's impossible to estimate the precise length of a bull run since market dynamics are impacted by several variables, and they may change swiftly.

Chapter 3

How Prepared Are You?

Preparing for a prospective bull run season needs a mix of study, preparation, and risk management knowledge. Here are some basic tips:

- Research and Stay Informed: - Understand market patterns and variables that might impact a bull run. Stay informed on key news, economic statistics, and changes in the financial world.

- Diversify Your Portfolio: - Spread your assets across several asset classes to lessen risk. Diversification may help grab opportunities in numerous areas during a bull market.

- Set Clear Objectives: - Define your investing objectives and risk tolerance. Establish a clear entry and exit strategy for your assets.

- Risk Management: - Use stop-loss orders to reduce possible losses. Be wary of over-leveraging, and only invest what you can afford to lose.

- Examine and change: - Regularly examine and change your portfolio depending on shifting market circumstances. Stay flexible and be prepared to change your plan as required.

- Stay Disciplined: - Emotions may affect decision-making. Stick to your set approach, even if the market gets erratic.

- Keep Cash on Hand: - Having cash handy helps you to take advantage of purchasing opportunities during market falls.

- Professional Advice: - Consider speaking with a financial adviser who can give specialized counsel based on your financial condition and objectives.

  Remember, although planning is key, investing always entails risks, and there are no assurances in the financial markets. Always conduct your own research and make educated judgments based on your specific circumstances.

Position yourself now!!!

I can give broad information, but it's crucial to realize that forecasting market moves, even bull runs, may be very unexpected. Consider careful research, diversification, and being updated about market movements before making any financial choices. More significantly, place yourself in the crypto market amid other financial possibilities, the reason being that the crypto market has a charted path it follows from year to year, the bull run in the Crypto Market happens every four years following Bitcoin Halving.

You know, bull market values usually appear ridiculous in a bad market, A bull market prediction often refers to an anticipation or prognosis that the financial markets would have a protracted period of increasing asset prices. In a bull market, investor confidence is strong, and there's broad optimism about the future performance of stocks or other financial instruments. Predicting a bull market entails examining multiple economic data, market movements, and other elements to predict good market circumstances.

However, it's vital to approach market projections with care, since they are fundamentally unreliable and may be altered by unanticipated occurrences.

"No way $XXX coin can achieve that price! Lol"

THIS MIGHT WAKE SOMEONE UP FROM SLEEP HOPEFULLY.

In 2021 bull market......

$KDA grew from $0.31 to $28. A 9,000% pump in 100 days

$SOL witnessed a 50,000% surge from $0.50 to $263 at its height

$AXS went one better. by moving 132,000%! A change from $0.12 to $164

The 2017 bull market had some wild movements too.

$NEO blasted from $4.60 to $200 and increased by 4,200%

In only a few months, $ADA produced a 6,700% rise from 1 cent to $1.30

But probably the strangest action of all time occurred from $XVG.

At the beginning of 2017, $XVG was priced at $0.000019. at the conclusion of the year, it had surged to $0.30 per coin

That's a move of 1,582,000%. in 12 months!

So what does all this mean?

The 2024/2025 Bull run will be mind-blowing!!!

Chapter 4

Notable Crypto Terms To Note

For beginners, here are some significant Crypto acronyms, you'll likely come across;

TP = Take-Profit

SL = Stop-Loss

B/E = Breakeven

FOMO = Fear Of Missing Out

BTD = Buy The Dip

CT = Crypto Twitter

ATH / ATL = All-Time High / All-Time Low

FUD = Fear, Uncertainty, Doubt

KYC = Know Your Customer

NFT = Non-Fungible Token

ROI = Return On Investment

HODL = Hold On for Dear Life

DYOR = Do Your Own Research

DEFI = Decentralized Finance

SAFU = Safe

HTF = Higher Time Frame

LTF = Lower Time Frame

PNL = Profit n Loss

IMO = In My Opinion

NFA = Not A Financial Advice

AMA= Ask Me Anything

CEX = Centralized Exchange

DEX = Decentralized Exchange

Chapter 5
Diverse Crypto Opportunities

1). Mining

Crypto mining is the process of confirming transactions on a blockchain and adding them to the public ledger, known as the blockchain. Miners utilize powerful computers to solve complicated mathematical problems, and when they correctly solve a problem, they add a new block to the blockchain and are rewarded with freshly produced cryptocurrency coins. This method is vital for ensuring the integrity and security of numerous cryptocurrencies, such as Bitcoin.

Mining is the most frequent technique to generate money using crypto. Mining validates transactions on the blockchain and adds fresh blocks of data to the network. By doing this, miners are rewarded with bitcoin for their labor. Mining may be done with specialist gear or using cloud mining services. You don't need to acquire or maintain gear with cloud mining, but you simply need to focus on daily mining.

2). Crypto Airdrops

Crypto airdrops refer to the release of free cryptocurrency tokens or coins to a large number of wallet addresses. This is typically done by blockchain projects or corporations to boost awareness, reward existing users, or encourage involvement in a new platform. Airdrops can be scheduled and receivers often need to fulfill certain requirements, such as possessing a specific cryptocurrency or being part of a particular community, to qualify for the free tokens. This might possibly generate money in various ways:

i. *Free Tokens*: In a typical airdrop, cryptocurrency projects issue free tokens to holders of a certain coin or to users who match certain requirements. If you obtain these tokens, they have the potential to rise in value over time.

ii. *New Project Opportunities*: Airdrops typically encourage new blockchain projects. If the project succeeds and the tokens acquire value, the tokens you received for free might become valuable assets.

iii. *Participation and Engagement*: Some airdrops demand you to connect with the initiative, such as joining their social media channels or recommending others. By engaging, you may earn more tokens or incentives.

iv. *Staking and Governance*: Airdropped coins may have usefulness inside the project's ecosystem. They may be used for staking to receive rewards or for participating in governance choices, letting you earn additional tokens.

v. *Selling or Trading*: Once you have airdropped tokens, you may opt to sell or trade them on cryptocurrency exchanges. If the token acquires popularity and demand, its price may climb, letting you benefit.

However, it's crucial to exercise caution: - Not all airdrops are authentic; some may be hoaxes.

- Airdropped tokens might sometimes be useless or have no practical utility.

- You may need to pay taxes on any earnings from airdropped tokens, depending on your country's tax rules.

Before participating in a crypto airdrop, investigate the project, read the terms and circumstances, and be wary about revealing personal information. Airdrops can be a means to possibly generate money in the crypto industry, but they also come with hazards.

3). Crypto Gaming

Crypto gaming, also known as blockchain gaming, includes the integration of blockchain technology and cryptocurrencies into video games. In crypto gaming, in-game assets and transactions are frequently stored on a blockchain, enabling players with actual ownership and provable scarcity of virtual things. Cryptocurrencies or blockchain-based tokens may be utilized as in-game currency or awards, and smart contracts on the blockchain can manage features like ownership, transfers, and trading of virtual assets. This integration of gaming with blockchain technology seeks to provide transparency, security, and new business models to the gaming sector.

Crypto gaming rewards players with cryptocurrency or NFTs that they own when they earn them and may maybe swap for stablecoins or fiat cash.

4). ICOs

An Initial Coin Offering (ICO) is a fundraising strategy utilized by blockchain and cryptocurrency businesses to obtain funds. In an ICO, the project offers its own native cryptocurrency tokens to investors in return for known cryptocurrencies like Bitcoin or Ethereum, or occasionally fiat money.

Investors join in the ICO with the assumption that the project's tokens will acquire value after the platform or product is constructed and launched. It's vital to note that ICOs have attracted regulatory attention owing to possible fraud and lack of investor protection. Some governments have enacted rules to control ICOs, while others have outlawed or limited them. As a result, various fundraising strategies, such as Security Token Offerings (STOs) and Initial Exchange Offerings (IEOs), have gained appeal as more legal alternatives.

ICOs often entail the issue of a new cryptocurrency token that will be utilized inside the project's ecosystem. The procedure is analogous to an initial public offering (IPO) in the traditional financial markets but is particular to the Bitcoin world. Initial Coin Offerings (ICOs) are a sort of investment that involves buying a company's token issued in exchange for cryptocurrency. ICOs are a terrific method to make money using crypto, as they may provide substantial returns on your investment. However, it's necessary to be aware of the hazards associated. Many ICOs are frauds and can result in losses, so confirm the ICO is authentic before investing.

5). **Investing**

Investing in Bitcoin is a terrific approach to making money using crypto. You may invest in individual currencies, like as Bitcoin and Ethereum, or you can participate in a cryptocurrency index fund. This is an excellent method to diversify your portfolio and spread your risk. When investing in cryptocurrencies, make it a point to study and comprehend the dangers you will take.

6). **Staking**

Crypto staking is a way of investing in cryptocurrencies that requires keeping a specified quantity of coins in your wallet for a certain duration. By doing this, you are rewarded with a small interest in your investment. So, you may make passive income from your crypto assets. The interest you can earn depends on the cryptocurrency and the quantity of coins you are staking. Some cryptocurrencies provide bigger incentives than others, so it's vital to conduct your homework first.

7. **Yield Farming**

Yield farming in the crypto sector refers to the activity of using various decentralized finance (DeFi) protocols and services to optimize profits on bitcoin holdings. Participants, known as yield farmers, supply liquidity to these protocols by lending or staking their crypto assets in return for incentives. The benefits of yield farming generally come in the form of additional tokens or interest payments. This approach allows users to make a passive income on their Bitcoin holdings while actively engaging in the decentralized financial ecosystem.

Yield farming may be difficult and entails traversing numerous DeFi platforms, knowing various protocols, and managing risks connected with smart contract vulnerabilities and market swings. It has gained popularity as a technique for crypto investors to produce additional profits beyond typical approaches like holding and trading. However, it also comes with hazards, and participants should properly investigate and understand the projects they engage with in the yield farming process.

Cryptocurrency can let you earn interest on your assets. It is done through a " yield farming process," where you lend your Bitcoin to a platform in return for a payout. The amount of dividend you get will totally depend on the site and the sort of bitcoin you are lending.

There are several sites offering yield farming options, but not all of them are secure or dependable. So, choose the trustworthy ones.

8). Lending

Cryptocurrency lending is another way to commercialize crypto. It entails lending your Bitcoin to someone else in exchange for interest. The interest rate you receive will depend on the type of cryptocurrency you are lending and the quantity you are financing.

9). Crypto Trading

Crypto trading is purchasing and selling cryptocurrencies in the financial markets with the intention of generating a profit. Traders engage in cryptocurrency markets on numerous platforms, such as cryptocurrency exchanges. The basic purpose is to capitalize on price variations of different cryptocurrencies.

There are two primary forms of crypto trading:

1. **Spot Trading**: In spot trading, traders purchase and sell real cryptocurrencies like Bitcoin, Ethereum, or other altcoins. The transaction is resolved "on the spot," meaning the delivery of the cryptocurrency happens instantaneously.

2. **Derivatives Trading:** This entails trading financial items whose value is generated from the underlying cryptocurrency. Examples include futures contracts and options. Derivatives allow traders to bet on the price swings of cryptocurrencies without owning the underlying assets.

Crypto Trading is the most common technique to generate money using crypto. This includes purchasing and selling cryptocurrencies on a crypto exchange. You may take advantage of the price changes and benefit by doing so. Crypto trading needs knowing market analysis, technical analysis, and risk management. Traders utilize diverse tactics, including day trading, swing trading, and long-term investment, to manage the turbulent cryptocurrency markets. It's vital for traders to keep educated on market trends, news, and regulatory events that might affect the value of cryptocurrencies.

Note that trading cryptocurrencies is hazardous and can result in losses. Therefore, master your basics before you start trading.

10). **Affiliate Programs**

Many cryptocurrency exchanges provide affiliate programs allowing you to earn money on suggested consumers. By recommending consumers to an exchange, you can earn a portion of the transaction fees they pay. It is a terrific method to generate money with crypto without having to perform any trading or investment. Affiliate programs may be quite competitive, so list down your greatest findings. Many amazing affiliate programs are accessible on the market, so investigate and locate the most profitable ones.

Chapter 6

Risk Management

Risk management is the first tactic any new trader has to master, but is frequently disregarded until it's too late. While bull markets might bring profit possibilities, they are not without hazards. Prudent risk management, including diversification and placing stop-loss orders, is vital. Remember that investing in cryptocurrencies includes risks, and previous performance is not indicative of future outcomes. It's essential to contact a financial expert before making any investment choices, particularly in the dynamic and fast-changing cryptocurrency market.

It's a financial advice to only invest what you can afford to lose in the Bull Run market. The notion of "only invest what you can afford to lose" is a typical piece of risk management advice, however, it's crucial to highlight that this statement doesn't represent customized financial advice. Manage your risk successfully by assessing how much you can afford to risk on your entire investment and then stick to it.

Follow this up by determining how much you can afford to lose on each particular transaction and then stick to it by setting a stop-loss order to minimize your losses when the market goes against you. Support these techniques by avoiding emotional decision-making and creating an investing strategy that includes target entry and exit prices. While it's crucial to be current with news and market occurrences, attempt to minimize your use of social media which may sometimes be full of exaggeration and push you to be greedy. It's a basic guideline aimed to underline the inherent dangers connected with investing.

Here's why this idea is commonly emphasized:
1. **Risk Awareness:**- Investing always entails risks, and the value of assets might vary. Acknowledging the danger of losing the invested cash helps investors make more informed judgments.

2. **Market Uncertainty:** - Financial markets may be unpredictable, and several variables, including economic circumstances, geopolitical events, and market mood, can affect asset values unexpectedly.

3. **Protecting Financial Well-Being:** - Investing money that you can afford to lose helps safeguard your overall financial well-being. It guarantees that critical living expenditures and other financial commitments are not compromised by prospective investment losses.

4. **Emotional Resilience:** - Acknowledging the likelihood of losses might lead to emotional resilience. If assets drop in value, investors who are psychologically prepared for this eventuality are less likely to make rash choices based on fear or panic.

5. **Long-Term Perspective:** - Having the mentality of "only invest what you can afford to lose" generally fosters a more long-term approach. It may help investors weather short-term market volatility without making hasty judgments.

It's vital for people to analyze their personal financial status, risk tolerance, and investing objectives before making any investment selections. Consulting with a financial adviser may give specialized recommendations based on particular circumstances.

Remember that investing is a personal choice, and different people have differing risk tolerances and financial conditions. While the idea is a smart guideline, it's not a one-size-fits-all rule, and people should examine their own particular circumstances when making investment selections.

Market dynamics that might affect a bull run

Several market movements might impact the potential of a bull run. Keep in mind that forecasting market moves is inherently unpredictable, but here are some elements to consider:

1. **Economic Growth:** - Strong economic indicators, such as GDP growth, low unemployment, and strong consumer mood, frequently contribute to a bullish market.

2. **Corporate Earnings:** - Robust corporate earnings reports may improve investor confidence and propel stock prices upward.

3. **Interest Rates:** - Low-interest rates may boost borrowing and spending, encouraging economic development and even propelling a bull market.

4. Central Bank Policies: - Accommodative monetary policies, where central banks give stimulus and assistance, may generate ideal circumstances for a bull market.

5. Technological breakthroughs: - Innovations and breakthroughs in technology may promote development in certain industries, leading to a larger market rally.

6. Global Political Stability: - A stable geopolitical climate may increase investor confidence and contribute to a favorable market mood.

7. Positive Earnings Expectations:- Forward-looking optimism about future profits and company prospects may stimulate investment and fuel a bull market.

8. Inflationary Environment: - Moderate inflation levels are frequently regarded as desirable for economic development and might be helpful to a bull market.

9. Favorable Regulatory Environment: -Policies that boost corporate development and eliminate regulatory uncertainty may favorably benefit the markets.

10. **Investor optimism:** - Positive optimism among investors, expressed in purchasing activity and risk-taking, may contribute to a positive market.

It's vital to recognize that these trends are interrelated, and market dynamics are driven by a complex interaction of many elements. Monitoring these patterns and remaining updated about global economic circumstances may help investors estimate the possibility of a bull run, but it's vital to approach market forecasts with care and weigh possible hazards.

Distribution of your investments across several classes helps decrease possible Risk in the Bull Run Market.

Here are techniques on diversification:

1. **Stocks:** - Invest in a variety of different stocks from diverse industries to prevent concentration risk. Consider both growth and value stocks for a balanced strategy.

2. **Bonds:** - Allocate a part of your portfolio to bonds, which are often less volatile than equities. Diversify bond investments among government, corporate, and municipal bonds.

3. **Real Estate:** - Real estate investments, such as real estate investment trusts (REITs), may offer diversity and income.

4. **Commodities:** - Include commodities like gold, silver, or other commodities in your portfolio to hedge against inflation and diversify risk.

5. **Cash or Cash Equivalents:** - Keep a part of your portfolio in cash or cash equivalents to have liquidity and take advantage of chances during market swings.

6. **International Investments:** - Consider exposure to international markets to lessen dependency on a single country's economic success.

7. **Other Investments:** - Explore other investments like hedge funds or private equity to offer extra diversity.

8. **Sector Diversification:** - Within each asset class, diversify across multiple sectors. For example, inside stocks, have exposure to technology, healthcare, finance, etc.

9. **Risk Tolerance Assessment:** - Align your asset allocation with your risk tolerance and investing objectives. Adjust the combination depending on your comfort level with risk.

10. **Rebalance Regularly:** - Periodically assess your portfolio and rebalance to preserve the appropriate asset allocation. This entails selling assets that have performed well and purchasing those that are underperforming. Remember that diversification doesn't guarantee profits or protect against losses, particularly in severe market situations. It's crucial to regularly analyze and alter your portfolio depending on changing market circumstances, economic trends, and your personal financial ambitions.

Utilizing stop-loss orders to reduce possible losses in the Bull Run Market.

Using stop-loss orders is a risk management approach that may help reduce possible losses during a bull market. How to can deploy stop-loss orders effectively:

1. **Setting Clear Stop-Loss Levels:** - Determine the highest loss you are ready to bear on a given investment. This is your stop-loss level.

2. **Technical Analysis:** - Use technical analysis, such as support levels or moving averages, to identify crucial places at which you may wish to position your stop-loss orders.

3. **Volatility Consideration:** - Take into consideration the volatility of the asset. More volatile assets may need greater stop-loss margins to prevent being triggered too quickly.

4. **Risk-Reward Ratio:** - Assess the risk-reward ratio for each transaction. A frequent strategy is to establish stop-loss levels at a position where the possible loss is acceptable in comparison to the predicted benefits.

5. **Periodically Update Stop-Loss Orders:** - As the market moves and prices fluctuate, periodically examine and update your stop-loss orders to match the current market circumstances.

6. **Discipline and Automation:** - Implement stop-loss orders methodically and adhere to them. Emotional judgments during market volatility might lead to uneven risk management.

7. **Trailing Stop-Loss Orders:** - Consider utilizing trailing stop-loss orders, which automatically adjust when the market price advances in your favor. This helps lock in earnings while also guarding against unexpected downturns.

8. **Market circumstances:** - Be cognizant of market circumstances. In a quickly rising market, raising stop-loss levels to capture profits while guarding against large downturns becomes critical.

9. **Diversification:** - Avoid focusing too much wealth on a single venture. Diversification helps lessen the effect of a possible loss on your total portfolio.

10. **Stay Informed:** - Keep updated on news and happenings that may affect the market. Sudden changes might generate volatility, and being aware helps in making prompt judgments.

General Tips On Crypto Investment
Cryptocurrency investments are extremely speculative and may be volatile. Before investing in crypto, undertake comprehensive research and determine your risk tolerance. Here are some tips:

1. **Research:** - Understand the basics and technology underlying the cryptocurrency you are considering. Investigate the development team, use case, collaborations, and community support.

2. **Diversification:** - Diversify your crypto holdings to spread risk. Avoid placing all your savings into a single coin.

3. **Long-Term View:** - Consider a long-term investing viewpoint rather than attempting to time the market. Cryptocurrency markets may be exceedingly unpredictable.

4. **Risk Management:** - Only invest what you can afford to lose. Cryptocurrency markets may see huge price changes.

5. **Stay Updated:** - stay abreast of the latest news and advancements in the domain of crypto. Market sentiment may be impacted by legislative changes, technical improvements, and macroeconomic reasons.

6. **Security:** - Prioritize the security of your assets. Use trustworthy wallets and exchanges, activate two-factor authentication, and investigate cold storage solutions for long-term holdings.

7. **Regulatory Considerations:** - Be informed of the regulatory landscape for cryptocurrencies in your area. Regulations may affect the market and your ability to buy/sell particular currencies.

8. **Community and Social Media**: - Engage with the Bitcoin community and remain updated via reliable social media outlets. However, be aware of the hype and perform your own due investigation.

What To Expect In A Bull Run

During a crypto bull run, certain expectations typically arise:

1. **Rising values:** The major expectation is for the values of cryptocurrencies to climb dramatically, occasionally reaching new all-time highs.

2. **Increased Trading Activity:** Bull runs often correspond with larger trading volumes as more investors participate in the market, both buying and selling.

3. **Market Optimism:** Bull runs promote a sense of optimism and confidence among investors, leading to positive sentiment and a readiness to take on greater risk.

4. **FOMO (Fear of Missing Out):** As prices climb, there's typically a fear of missing out on possible profits, prompting more investors to enter the market.

5. **Media Attention:** Bull runs tend to draw media attention, with mainstream sites reporting the spike in bitcoin prices and associated stories.

6. **Altcoin Rally:** While Bitcoin frequently leads the bull run, numerous other cryptocurrencies (altcoins) also enjoy strong price rises, often outpacing Bitcoin.

7. **Increasing Adoption:** Bull runs may correlate with increasing adoption of cryptocurrencies, both among individual investors and institutions, as they seek exposure to the growing market.

8. **Speculative Behavior:** Bull markets may sometimes lead to speculative behavior, with some investors making riskier bets or investing in initiatives with little intrinsic value.

It's crucial to recognize that although bull runs may produce excitement and possible rewards, they are also accompanied by heightened volatility and the danger of rapid declines. As such, investors should approach bull markets with caution and perform rigorous research before making investing choices.

A bull market is often characterized by increasing asset values, a bullish investor mood, and an overall bullish view of the financial markets. During a bull run, many investors enjoy gains as the value of their assets grows. However, it's vital to understand that investing always entails risks, and previous performance is not indicative of future outcomes. Potential earnings in a bull market may come from numerous asset types, such as stocks, cryptocurrencies, real estate, and others. Investors who make well-timed and knowledgeable investing selections during a bull run may realize big profits.

It's vital, nevertheless, to approach investments with a realistic perspective and consider the following:

1. **Market Timing:** - Timing the market is tough. Investors should avoid attempting to forecast the precise top of a bull market or the bottom of a down market.

2. **Long-Term Perspective:** - A long-term investing strategy is frequently more sustainable than seeking to profit from short-term market changes.

3. **Investigate:** - Thoroughly investigate and comprehend the assets you are investing in. Fundamental research, technical analysis, and education about market movements are crucial.

4. **Individual Circumstances:** - Consider your individual financial objectives, risk tolerance, and investment horizon. What works for one investor may not be good for another.

Keep in mind that markets are fundamentally unpredictable, and there are no certainties in investing. While bull markets might present profit possibilities, it's vital to approach them with a well-thought-out plan and a realistic grasp of the accompanying dangers.

The timing of the Bull Run is a frequently asked question. Predicting the precise time of a bull run in financial markets, including cryptocurrency markets, is tough and frequently impossible. Bull runs are defined by protracted periods of increasing asset values, often driven by optimistic market mood, strong economic data, and other favorable circumstances. Market fluctuations are impacted by a number of variables, including economic data, geopolitical events, regulatory changes, and investor emotion, among others. These elements are dynamic and may change swiftly, making it difficult to identify the precise date of a bull run.

Instead of attempting to time the market perfectly, it's typically recommended to concentrate on long-term investing plans, do extensive research, diversify your portfolio, and keep updated about key market developments. Additionally, implementing risk management measures, such as establishing stop-loss orders, may help preserve your assets during moments of market volatility. If you are contemplating joining the market or modifying your investing strategy, it's vital to do so based on a well-thought-out plan and your particular financial objectives and risk tolerance.

Always be skeptical of anybody claiming to properly anticipate market timing, since it's intrinsically unreliable. The ideal time to purchase cryptocurrencies hasn't always been during the bull run.? The phrase "bull run" as earlier defined refers to a time in financial markets when asset values, including cryptocurrencies, show continuous upward momentum. While a bull market might bring the potential for profit, it's vital to approach cryptocurrency investments with cautious deliberation, and the timing of purchases should be dependent on individual circumstances and financial objectives.

Here are some items to consider:

1. **Study:** - Conduct a comprehensive study on the cryptocurrencies you are interested in. Understand the technology, use case, development team, and possibility for future adoption.

2. **Market Timing:** - Timing the market may be tricky. Instead of attempting to forecast short-term swings, consider a long-term investing plan based on research.

3. **Diversification:** - Diversify your bitcoin assets to spread risk. Avoid placing all your savings into a single coin.

4. **Risk Management:** - Set defined risk management methods, including stop-loss orders, to safeguard your assets from major downturns. Only invest what you can afford to lose. Cryptocurrency markets may see huge price changes.

5. **Regulatory Environment:** - Be informed of the regulatory environment for cryptocurrencies in your area. Regulatory changes might alter market sentiment.

6. **Long-Term View:** - Consider a long-term view rather than attempting to profit on short-term price swings. Cryptocurrency markets may be exceedingly volatile.

It's vital to understand that cryptocurrency investments entail inherent risks, and prices may be impacted by several variables, including market mood, technology improvements, regulatory changes, and macroeconomic situations. While a bull market may create ideal circumstances for price appreciation, it's also crucial to be careful and not succumb to FOMO (fear of missing out).

Evaluate your risk tolerance, establish realistic goals, and only invest what you can afford to lose. Remember that the information presented here is not financial advice. It's essential to speak with a financial professional for specialized recommendations based on your unique circumstances.

Chapter 7

The Future And The Bull Run

The occurrence of a crypto bull run is not intrinsically futuristic, since it is a phenomenon that has been witnessed throughout the history of cryptocurrency markets. However, the ramifications of a bull run and the greater use and growth of cryptocurrencies might be deemed futuristic in the sense that they reflect developments in technology, banking, and global economic systems. The potential for cryptocurrencies to alter established financial institutions, promote decentralized applications, and transform many sectors indicates a future view. Additionally, the innovation and experimentation within the cryptocurrency field, such as the development of blockchain technology, smart contracts, and decentralized finance (DeFi), add to a forward-thinking narrative.

Overall, although the notion of a bull run itself is not futuristic, the larger implications and possibilities of cryptocurrencies and blockchain technology coincide with future trends in technology and finance.

The cryptocurrency bull run is not always a one-off occurrence, it doesn't happen once and then terminates. It's recurring according to its timing and chart algorithm. Bull runs may occur several times over the lifespan of a coin or the whole cryptocurrency market. They are often driven by many variables such as market cycles, investor mood, adoption patterns, and external events. While bull runs are not guaranteed to repeat consistently or with the same amplitude, they are a recurrent occurrence in the cryptocurrency market, reflecting the dynamic character of the asset class and the shifting landscape of variables impacting its price.

Chapter 8

20 Must Have Coins in your Crypto Portfolio

With my years of knowledge in the crypto space, I can confidently say that these 20 coins I am providing you as a bonus for buying this book are all you need to become a millionaire or a billionaire, depending on your volume of purchases. These crypto gems have been extensively researched technically, with huge projects backing them up. Do well to acquire them from several crypto exchanges e.g. Binance, Trust Wallet, etc. You can do research on how to purchase them.

In conclusion, this is not financial advice, Always keep in mind that the liquid market is volatile and forecasts may not always be as promised.

<u>My precious bonus of 20 Coins to invest in are:</u>

1. Bitcoin

2. Avalanche

3. RDNT (Radiant)

4. Pepe

5. Arbitrum

6. The Internet Computer (ICP)

7. Solana

8. Sui

9. NEXA

10. Matic

11. CAW

12. Bonk

13. Chain Link

14. Doge chain

15. Meer

16. Minu

17. Lunc

18. DogeCoin

19. Shiba Inu

20. TKC

I wish to congratulate you ahead and welcome you personally to your next level of financial shift leveraging on Crypto with intentional preparation for this coming Crypto Bull Run. May I submit to you that this book is topical and the time to act is NOW.

SEE YOU ON TOP.